08724
STRAND PRICE
$ 5.00

W9-CLE-928

For darling Alan, and my two
lovely children, Harriet and Tom

First published in the United States 1991
by Dial Books for Young Readers
A Division of Penguin Books USA Inc.
375 Hudson Street
New York, New York 10014
Published in Great Britain
by Frances Lincoln Limited

Text copyright © 1990 by Frances Lincoln Limited
Photographs copyright © 1990 by Anthea Sieveking
All rights reserved
Printed in Mexico
First Edition
10 9 8 7 6 5 4 3

Library of Congress Cataloging in Publication Data
Sieveking, Anthea.
What color?: photographs / by Anthea Sieveking.
p.   cm.
Summary: Brief text and photographs display a variety
of colored objects familiar to babies.
ISBN 0-8037-0909-9:
1. Color—Juvenile literature. [1. Color. 2. Vocabulary.]
I. Title
QC495.5.S54   1991   535.6—dc20   90-43412   CIP   AC

WHAT COLOR?

Photographs by Anthea Sieveking

Dial Books for Young Readers · New York

What color is
Chiau Pheng's
raincoat?

Red

rainhat

raincoat

umbrella

boots

What color is Louis's balloon?

Orange

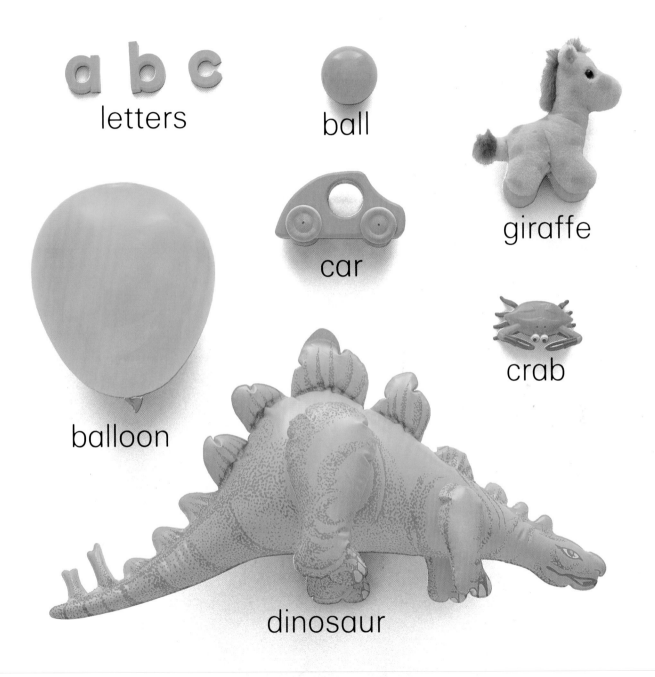

letters

ball

giraffe

balloon

car

crab

dinosaur

What color is Sabrina's shampoo?

Yellow

toothbrush

boat

shampoo

duck

sponge

soap

washcloth

What color is Daniel's apple?

Green

apple

peas

green pepper

beans

lettuce

zucchini

What color is Grace's cup?

Blue

spoon

fork

cup

bunny

plate

What color is Jessica's pig?

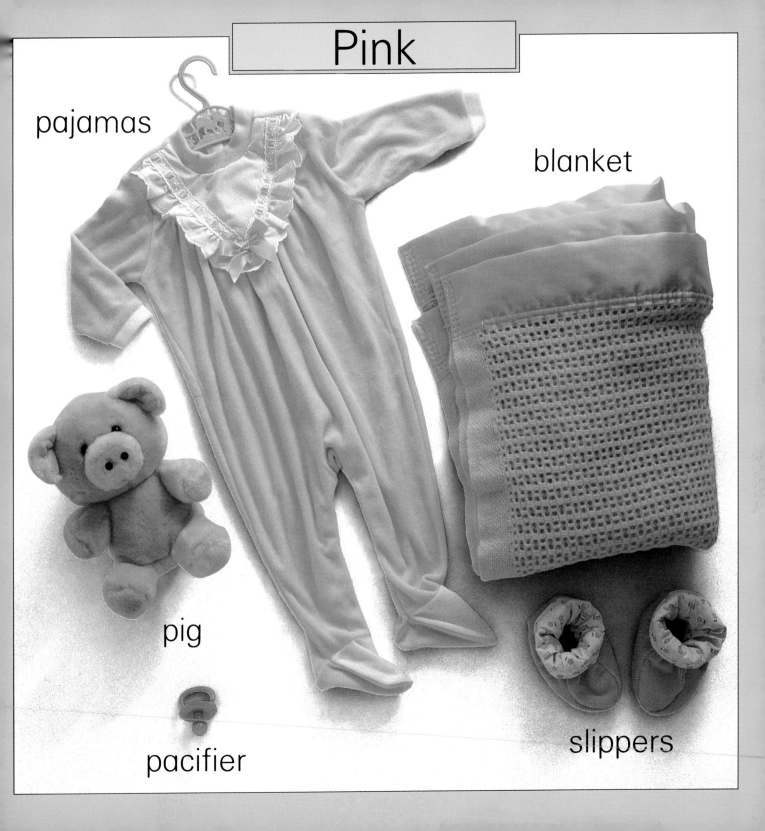

Pink

pajamas

blanket

pig

pacifier

slippers

What color are Sophie's and Zoe's hats?

Black

cat

gloves

necklace

hat

Daddy's shoes

What color is Lorelle's teddy bear?

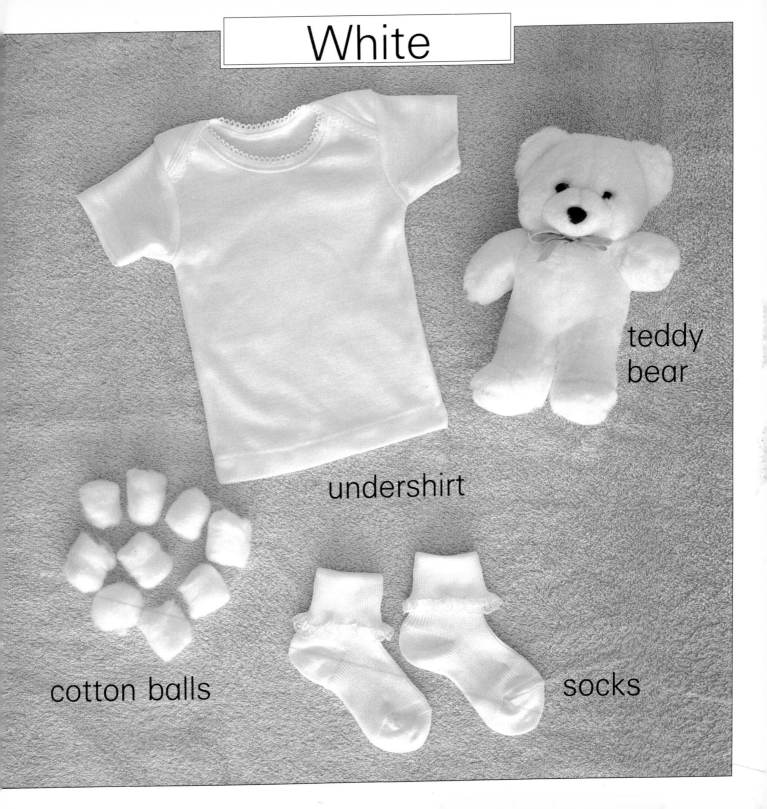

White

undershirt

teddy
bear

cotton balls

socks